with
ALL MY
HEART

This study belongs to:

TABLE *of* CONTENTS

INTRO

As a 30-year-old unmarried woman, in the South no less, I went through the frustrating times that singleness can bring. When looking for resources to guide me on this journey, I really wanted something that would actually make me feel lucky to be a single woman and get me excited about the unique opportunity that I had in front of me, but I never found it. The more I looked around, the more I saw that single women seemed to be mostly characterized by sadness and waiting. Waiting to be married, waiting to be fulfilled, and ultimately waiting for life to start. Unfortunately, what I saw was that for some, singleness meant not truly living life, but instead being in a holding state until prince charming came along.

Because there weren't a ton of encouraging books out there, I instead found myself digging into the scriptures and to my surprise, the Lord spoke so much truth to me about the single life through it. With these truths in mind, my single years turned into some of the best years of my life so far. My prayer for you is that you would experience the same thing and not miss another minute of "the GOOD single life". It exists! I promise :)

I'm not a theologian. I didn't go to seminary, and I haven't had a perfect record in my dating relationships. I'm just a regular girl, who went from questioning God and struggling that this was the path for my life, to living a life surrendered, hopeful, joyful, and closer to the Lord than ever before. This is my prayer for you as well! This can be a sweet, sweet time for you to be devoted solely to your heavenly Father, become more like Jesus, and show the Kingdom to God's people.

You never know how long your season of singleness will last. It may be another few months, another few years, or a lifetime, but the time will pass. Will you look back and regret what you did in this season? Or will you remember it as an intimate time that you squeezed out every ounce of goodness the Lord had for you? I'm thinking since you've picked this devotional up, it will be the latter :)

my PRAYER

I COME *before You now, with full faith and knowledge that You are a good God and that your plans for me are higher than my plans.*

I PRAY *that You would show me glimpses of Your plan to encourage me when I need it most.*

I PRAY *that all confidence I have would come from who I am in You.*

I PRAY *that You would surround me with the love of friends and family when I am lonely.*

I PRAY *for Your strength to push aside all the pressures of this world, so I can focus on what matters in Your eyes.*

I PRAY *that I would not only accept this season, but embrace it, thrive in it, and live it to it's fullest.*

I GIVE *You my entire life to do with as You see fit. I place it in Your hands to use me and my future in a way that would most benefit Your kingdom.*

I PRAY *that if a husband is in my future that You would be with him and guide him in all that he does. I pray that we would both be growing daily to become more and more like You and when the time comes we would follow You together.*

I PRAY *most importantly that I will pursue You Lord, with my whole heart, for the rest of my life.*

IN JESUS NAME, AMEN

TIPS &
REMINDERS

1. DO WORK THROUGH THE STUDY WITH A FRIEND.
If you don't know anyone going through, come join our online group!
You can ask questions or share any insight you receive as you go
through! Search *Wholehearted Ladies* on facebook.

2. DON'T SKIP THE SCRIPTURE READINGS!
The bible verses are gold and what I've found to be the most powerful
aspect of this study leading to life change.
A note about Versions of the Bible : I selected different versions of the Bible
that spoke to me most, but it's not imperative that you use that version! Also,
remember that The Message is a paraphrase of the Bible and not a word for
word translation. It's great as secondary resource and can bring a freshness
to verses that we have become very familiar with, but it's best not to use
paraphrased translations as your main study bible.

3. DO START WITH PRAYER AND BE EXPECTANT.
Ask the Holy Spirit to open your eyes to new truths and ask the Lord
to meet with you. Go into this believing that you will see Him and
His truth in a new way and that your life will never be the same.

4. DON'T THINK OF THIS AS HOMEWORK.
This is so much more than that! It is meant to be a tool that will
bring you into the presence of the Lord, if only you let it!

5. DO SHARE ON SOCIAL MEDIA!
My hope is that we will share a fresh new voice for the single
woman and with this voice, create a thriving community that will
change how others view singles and singleness.

6. DON'T FEEL LIKE YOU HAVE TO STAY ON TRACK.
If God is speaking, spend some time sitting with Him and listening
for His voice. No hurry or pressure to keep up! This whole study is
about not living on anyone's timeline but your own, remember? :)

Daily Devotions

LET'S DIG
DEEP FOR
TRUTH

one

THE MIND

Forget everything you have been taught about singleness from the world's perspective. It's probably not very good stuff anyway. Let's start with a blank slate and build our views on the truth in God's Word. We have been taught by the world to give way too much control to our emotions, but let's decide not to operate strictly from how we feel. Let's live our lives based on the words from the mouth of God.

Over the last year and a half, I have been reading through the Bible and I can't begin to tell you all the difference it has made in my life. Being able to saturate my mind in the Word of God is such a gift and has so much more transformative power than I sometimes realize. Through it we can learn so much about who God is. From the Old Testament, learning about His faithfulness, provision, and purpose to the New Testament where we get to see fulfillment of His promises with the birth and ministry of Jesus and the beginnings of the Church. Even though the events of the Bible happened long ago, it is still so relevant to our lives, and once we really dig in, we will begin to see that.

As we read, we have to remember, that we are not alone in this transformation! As Christians, we have received the Holy Spirit and the Holy Spirit gives us the power to know the mind of Christ. Because of this we can have confidence that we WILL be transformed as we read scripture and spend time with the Lord.

Thinking like the mind of Christ has the power to...
- bring you joy, peace, and understanding during the difficult times
- strengthen your faith when you can't see his plan
- help you see His plan
- make you more like Christ

13

When we think and act like Christ we have the power to really change our lives, but the mind is where it starts. We need to be intentional in seeking understanding of the mind of Christ and training ourselves to think like Him. It won't just happen automatically.

Anytime I have tried to change by my own strength, I have failed. If we simply change our actions without retraining our mind, the change will not stick. Focus on cultivating a mind like Christ and leave the results up to Him.

Transforming our mind to the mind of Christ is the first place to start and where lasting change begins.

THE WORD :

Romans 12:2 (ESV)   Philippians 4:8 (CEV)

2 Corinthians 10:5 (NLT)   1 Corinthians 2:12 (NLT)

Romans 8:6 (NIV)   Matthew 16:21-23 (CEV)

QUESTIONS :

1. What does God promise to those whose minds have been renewed?
2. How am I to know the mind of Christ?
3. What does Jesus call those who do not think like God? And what are they doing?
4. What lies do I believe that need to be confronted, so I can move forward living by God's truth?

Use the next few blank pages to work through the Scripture verses and answer these questions! Simply write out the verses, jot down main ideas or use the space to gather info from commentaries and other study tools.

two

WORLDLY

"THOSE THAT HAVE THEIR HEARTS FULL OF THIS WORLD …
HAVE A DEAF EAR TO THE GOSPEL."

Matthew Henry Commentary

If we were all in a room together right now, I'd ask you to share all the things that people have said to you about your singleness- some would probably be hilarious, but others might be hurtful. I'd share how when my twin sister was engaged I got asked probably one million times to see "my ring" or about how wedding planning was going. After she got married, it was always "Are you the married one?", which led to me feeling like "the other one". But I have no hate for those comments or the people who said them, cause let's be real here... the world has made us all believe that for 20-somethings, marriage is the holy grail.

There seems to be a general timeline for life that people have become accustomed to. When they meet someone who isn't on that track, it sort of makes people uncomfortable and they say things that can come off hurtful. (Side note, decide now not to be offended by every comment people make about your singlehood. It will make your life much easier and it's generally not their intention to offend anyway!) I remember telling my sister often "I'm cool with being single! I just wish everyone else was cool with me being single too!" My only solution, I thought, was to move to a big city where it was more socially acceptable to be single later in life, then I came across this little verse…

"The things that most people think are important are worthless as far as God is concerned." Luke 16:15b (CEV)

Call me crazy, but I think this is going to be my new life verse.

In this passage, Jesus is speaking about the Pharisees and their love of money, but I think we can apply this to anything the world puts too much emphasis on. People might not say it outright, but sometimes the judgy comments we hear tell of the underlying idea that if you are not married then you are missing out or there is something wrong with you. This can start to put a lot of pressure on you, but the world has it all wrong. Being married and having babies are not bad desires to have, but to say that these things are the goal of life is just not biblical. Until we realize that this isn't our goal for our time on earth, we will not only feel the pressure to have them, but we may even begin to feel entitled to these things. And when that happens disappointment will be sure to follow if these goals are not met.

It has become pretty clear to me that I cannot be swayed by what others think, no matter how many "others" I feel I am up against. Forget what the world thinks and release yourself from the pressure to live up to its timeline. The Lord is more concerned about the condition of my heart than my marital status. And I am more concerned with what He thinks about me than what the world thinks about me.

The world doesn't value the kingdom of God. Don't let it dictate how you feel about your singleness.

THE WORD :

1 Samuel 16:7 (NIV)   *1 John 5:4 (ESV)*
Galatians 1:10 (NIV)   *Luke 14:15-24 (NIV)*
2 Corinthians 10:3 (CEV)   *Hebrews 12:1 (NIV)*
1 John 2:15-17 (CEV)

QUESTIONS :

1. In what ways am I trying to win the approval of man?
2. Are there times that I have been like the invitees in the parable of the banquet- too full of the world to go to the Lord's table?
3. What worldly ideas or pressures do I need to "throw off" because they have been a hinderance to me?
4. Are there any streams of influence (social media, tv shows, etc.) that instigate negative feelings about singleness that I need to "throw off" so I can hear truth?

three

SEASONS

"FREEDOM COMES IN REALIZING THAT MARRIAGE AND
SINGLENESS ARE ROLES IN WHICH WE CARRY OUT A HIGHER
CALLING OF SERVING THE LORD, AND NOT PARTICULAR
CALLINGS IN AND OF THEMSELVES."

Fern Horst

I remember a friend, who was a mom, telling me she thought I had a glamorous single girl life. I was shocked. "Who me? But I'm not glamorous... Go on." She told me it was great that I got to have girls nights when I wanted to, wore makeup (This made me giggle! Surely I will continue to wear makeup even as a newlywed or mom! ;)), and had the freedom for adventure!!!

That conversation, though seemingly silly, opened up my eyes to a lot! There were opportunities that I was taking for granted, because I didn't realize that they might not always be around. My twin sister (who is married and birthed me my very best friends/ nieces) and I soon started a back and forth where we would say... "I'm jealous you get to 'fill in the blank'!" It started out as a joking thing, but I think it has helped both of us to recognize some things that we should be grateful for in the season we are in.

One thing that I have learned, through the heart-to-hearts with my married friends, is that all seasons have the good, but they also have the bad (or the cost). It's easy to see the pros of others' seasons, because that is what is put out there on display. But when we engage closely in the lives of others, you get to see the good times and the tough times, and hopefully we can learn from them. It's good to be realistic about different seasons, so that you don't become disillusioned with rose-colored glasses of desire for any one thing. This is one reason why comparison is so dangerous. We usually make comparisons based on what we think, rather than what is true.

Another thing that I have learned about seasons is that they only last for as long as the Lord allows. They are each gifts from God. Whether that is being a wife, a mother, or a career woman, you are not guaranteed to always have the gift you have been given. People lose jobs, spouses, and children. We would benefit from cherishing the time we have in any season, thanking the Lord for the blessings He has given, and using our unique situation to fulfill the calling He has on our lives.

Learning these two things about seasons has led me to appreciate where I am right now. I intentionally look for things to appreciate, whether it's a trip to Target alone (I hear that is a big one for moms) or just getting to have a super girly apartment, because I know that these are unique gifts that I may not always be able to enjoy.

Transforming our mind to the mind of Christ is the first place to start and where lasting change begins.

THE WORD :

Ecclesiastes 3:1 (CEV)   *James 4:13-15 (NIV)*
1 Thessalonians 5:18 (NIV)   *2 Timothy 4:2a (NIV)*

QUESTIONS :

1. What aspects of singleness am I grateful for?
2. What unique service to God's kingdom can I fulfill now, that I may not be able to do later?
3. Who has God put in my path that I can learn from? A wife? A mom? Ask the Lord to guide you in those friendships and that they would be a source of learning about other seasons.

four

DEPENDENCE

"[GOD] LIKES HIS KIDS COMPLETELY HANGING ON TO HIM FOR
DEAR LIFE MORE THAN HE CARES ABOUT THE PERFECT PLAN BEING
EXECUTED. HE IS AFTER US, AND UNCERTAINTY IS
USUALLY WHAT KEEPS US GLUED TO HIS SIDE."

Jennie Allen

I remember a time after my first real break-up where I was absolutely crushed. The Lord had told me clearly that I was not supposed to be with this guy, but to have all these hopes I had for a future just taken out from under me felt earth-shattering. It was the first time I really connected with this verse about the Bible and the fact that it was our DAILY bread. "Jesus answered, 'It is written: 'Man shall not live on bread alone, but by every word that comes from the mouth of God.'" – Luke 4:4.

There were times that I literally could not make it through the day without reading the Bible. When I'd start to feel depressed and cry, I'd pull out my Bible and just read. The moment I started reading, waves of peace and hope would come over me. Up until that point, I'd never spent much time with the Lord. I was desperate, but luckily the Lord didn't judge me for that or the fact that He was my last resort. He just wanted me to come to Him.

When people ask about the times I felt the closest to the Lord, it has always been without a doubt those months after a big break-up. (I've had a few! It has taken me quite a while to learn all this stuff. Make it easier on yourself and learn from my mistakes if you can!) It was during those times that I realized my joy could not be placed on anything other than God. It was such a sweet time of communion with the Lord, filled with intimacy with Him, hope for what He had for me, and faith beyond what I could see.

Unfortunately for some, it can take uncertainty in life to turn to the Lord. Sometimes it's not until we feel the loneliness, the worry about our future, or the biological clock ticking, before we come to Him as the ultimate supplier of all of our needs. It may be that your season of singleness is meant to draw you into a greater dependence on God. This is not to say that all singleness can be attributed to the Lord trying to get our attention, but it is a possibility and we need to be open to that. There are other possible reasons God has for singleness that we will discuss in a few chapters.

The truth is that every day of our life is uncertain, but for some reason we don't realize it if we have our "plan" on track or seem to have it all together, according to the world's standards. Our need for Him is always there, but we feel it during some times more than others, like singleness.

Dependence is a beautiful state where the Lord's glory shines. Our resources (or lack of resources) take a back seat to the Lord's, which are incomparable. Through acknowledgement of our weaknesses, we tap into the Lord's power and are the strongest we will ever be. So embrace your need for the Savior, look forward to all that He will do, and remember that when you are weak, He is strong.

When faced with uncertainty, we are given an opportunity to experience a dependence on the Father that makes us stronger than our strongest self. Use the opportunities to build a foundation of dependence on the only One who satisfies, and the only One who will never let you down.

THE WORD :

Matthew 5:3 (MSG) *Exodus 4:10-12 (CEV)*
Colossians 2:6-7 (NLT) *Jeremiah 17:5-8 (NIV)*
Psalms 62:5-6 (CEV) *2 Corinthians 12:8-10 (NLT)*

QUESTIONS :

1. What does the Bible promise to those who depend on God? And those who don't?
2. What would it look like to depend on the Lord more than I depend on others?
3. Are there any situations in my life right now that God might be using to get my attention?

five

THE GIFT GIVER

"I DELIGHT MYSELF IN YOU, IN THE GLORY OF YOUR PRESENCE,
I'M OVERWHELMED. I'M OVERWHELMED BY YOU."

———————————————— *Big Daddy Weave* ————————————————

One unfortunate side effect of singleness is the tendency to focus on what we have and what we have not. We do an inventory comparison of each person's gifts so to speak, and when we come up wanting, it begs the question "Why not me?". But we are called to shift our focus from the gifts to the Gift Giver. Once we do this we will realize that He is the only Gift we need.

How many of you want to close the book right now, because of how cliché that sounds? I would and probably have before with similar sentiments. But how much time do we spend thinking about what we don't have, all the while not realizing the Gift that is right in front of our face. I read a book called *Sacred Singleness* and I highly recommend it. (It's actually weird because I remember buying the Kindle version, because I didn't want anyone to know I bought a book on singleness and be labeled a "single girl"... and now I'm writing one, God's funny like that.) Throughout the book, she encourages us to seek the Lord's presence and enjoy the love story between us and the Father. It wasn't in a cliche way, like the "Jesus is my boyfriend" thing, but a true call to experience the great love we can enjoy by being close to the Lord and abiding in Him. It was then that I stopped praying for a list of things I desired and only prayed to experience His presence.

The song "Overwhelmed" by Big Daddy Weave, quoted above, soon became my anthem for my single season. The intimacy I encountered with the Lord was like nothing I had ever felt and I was truly overwhelmed to the point of tears very frequently as I sat in His presence. It wasn't all just an emotional thing though, I genuinely felt a weight off of my spirit and all I wanted was more of Him.

Months later when I started dating someone pretty seriously, I wrote in my journal to the Lord "I miss the intimacy that I shared with you while I was single and seeking you wholeheartedly. How do I get back to that place?". It shocked me. Don't get me wrong, I have definitely enjoyed my single years, but I never expected to miss those times so much that I'd want to go back.

It marked a season for me where His presence became the gift I most desired. When we take delight in experiencing the presence of God, we won't want to ever be without it and we won't be satisfied to look for other substitutes (or gifts).

Seek the face of the Gift Giver and not His gifts. You will be blessed in a much bigger way by who He is rather than by what He gives.

THE WORD :

1 Chronicles 16:10-11 (NIV)   *Psalm 27:4 (MSG)*
Psalm 119:37 (CEV)   *Psalm 73:28 (NLT)*
James 4:8a (NLT)   *Psalms 16 (CEV)*

QUESTIONS :

1. What does God promise to those who seek Him?
2. What gifts am I seeking over the Gift Giver?

six

CELEBRATE

8... # of weddings I was in over the course of 5 years
0... # of dates I had to those weddings

The memories of wedding weekends with all of my very best friends are honestly some of my greatest memories and my favorite times - even with no date! We danced all night, and I was able to give full attention to my best friend, with no random guy to babysit. Not only was putting aside my insecurities about my singleness and celebrating with the bride what she needed, but it always turned out to be just as much of a blessing to me! As I look back, I realize what grace it was that I was either not dating anyone at the time or that the guy I was "talking to" at the moment couldn't make it. I now see it only as God's favor that allowed me to be fully present, though it didn't seem like that at the time!

Believe me, I get it. It can be hard to go to showers, bachelorette parties, and weddings (even baby showers and hospital rooms for births) when you aren't at that same place in life. It can make you feel like you are behind the curve in life. At the very least it can just make you jealous that they get a whole house of new stuff and you're sitting over there with holes in your towels and dingy pots and pans.

It CAN make you feel all those things, but it doesn't have to. The joy of the celebration for others is sucked out when we become preoccupied with ourselves. It is a shame when our first response to hearing of another's blessing, is to think about our own situation. A friend's blessing should not highlight your lack, it should only highlight their gift and the Gift Giver.

During almost every rehearsal dinner speech by a bride and groom, they say how much they appreciate getting to share this time with those they love. Imagine if everyone decided to only celebrate with the couple if things were going well in their own lives. The Bible says to love others like we would love ourselves. How would we "love ourselves" if we were in their situation?

If marriage and babies is something you desire for your future, then it should make your heart happy for one of your friends to receive that gift. When we take our minds off ourselves, it is much easier to celebrate with others. Steer clear of the temptation to make it about you, choose to focus on your friend, think about yourself less and make fun memories, celebrating with your besties.

We are called to rejoice with those who rejoice. Let's remove ourselves from the equation and focus on others by celebrating the blessings of our loved ones.

THE WORD :

Proverbs 15:30 (ESV)   *Romans 12:15 (NIV)*
Psalm 118:24 (CEV)   *Galatians 5:14 (ESV)*
Philippians 2:3-4 (ESV)

QUESTIONS :

1. What does God promis to those who rejoice?
2. How do I picture the celebration surrounding my own wedding or child's birth?
3. Am I celebrating my friends like I want to be celebrated?
4. Is there anyone I need to support who is experiencing the blessings I desire?
5. What are so practical ways I can show love and support?

SILENCE

There were quite a few years that I like to call "the quiet years". It seemed like everyone had something going on at one time or another. Weddings, babies, new jobs, big moves, finding their calling for life and I was just kind of bored. I had a great job and family, but I didn't really feel like God was working in my life. I didn't feel far away from Him, but I didn't feel like I was being purposeful or being used by Him either.

Hindsight tells me differently. Hindsight tells me that He has been at work- hard at work, creating a beautiful story, behind the scenes of the life that was visible to me. There are so many circumstances that I had questioned the purpose of for so long, and now I can look back and see the purpose in them. I don't think we will always be able to look back and see so clearly what He was doing, but I do believe that He will let us have a glimpse of the big plan every once in a while, to strengthen our faith and keep us encouraged. Now when things seem hazy to me, I think back on all that God has done and it brings me a lot of peace to know that He was faithful then and will be faithful now.

Oh how I wished I could have just known at that time what the future held, then (I told myself) I could chill out and just enjoy life until I met Mr. Right. I could avoid the minefield that is dating until the time was right and if I KNEW I was going to be married one day then I would not need to worry myself with the possibility of never being a wife or mother. Um hello, Natalie, if that was the case then there would be no need for faith and reliance on God for my future. If I knew what the future held it wouldn't be necessary to ask God what I should do about a potential boyfriend or to pour out my fears to Him about possibly missing out on marriage and motherhood. I could have missed out on being comforted by my Father or learning that He alone is all I need.

So it seems that the quiet years actually turned out to be my strengthening years. What I learned over those years, in chasing after Him, has been so beneficial in my spiritual journey with the Lord and I will never look at silence the same again. I still won't always know what the purpose of every circumstance is, but I will thank God for the trial and look forward to one day getting a glimpse into what all the fuss was about!

God is always working even when we can't see it. Silence and waiting is an opportunity for our faith to grow.

THE WORD :

Deuteronomy 8:2 (NIV)
Lamentations 3:25 (ESV)
Lamentations 3:25-28 (CEV)
Matthew 4:1 (ESV)

Psalms 27:13-14 (NIV)
Hebrews 11:1 (NLT)
1 Peter 4:12-13 (MSG)

QUESTIONS :

1. What does the Bible say are possible reasons for silence?
2. What does God promise to those who wait?
3. When Jesus was tempted by the devil, where did it happen? Who else was with Him?
4. Write about a time when the Lord has been faithful to you in the past, that you can remember during the times when you cannot see the purpose.

FAITHFUL

I remember very often praying to God "I don't know your plan, but I know everything is in Your hands, and I thank you for this trial." I'm not sure how to explain it, but it had to only be by the strength of the Holy Spirit, because left to my own self, I wouldn't have always been able to pray that. Even in those times of confusion, and wondering what God was up to, I never doubted that His plan for me was best. Does that mean it was easy??? Heck, no. (My struggles had more to do with why it was like that for me and not for someone else ... But we will get to that later.)

If you're finding singleness to be a tough season fo you, just remember that the Lord is watching to see how you will respond. His desire is for us to love Him and be faithful to Him regardless of what He is doing for us. (And the truth is, just cause we don't see it, doesn't mean He is not working in our lives. We know that He is always at work.) His desire is for us to say "Yes, Father, whatever your will, I will not forsake you."

In reading through Daniel, I came across this verse "The God we worship can save us from you and your flaming furnace. But even if He doesn't, we still won't worship your gods and the gold statue you have set up." Daniel 3:17-18 (CEV)

Wow. Shadrach, Meshach and Abednego are threatened with death by a flaming furnace if they don't bow down to the false gods. They know their God is powerful enough to save them, but they also know that if He decides not to save them, then He has a better plan, and He is still worthy to alone be praised. I want a faith like that. I want a steady faith that does not waver based on my circumstances and a faith that knows beyond a shadow of a doubt that God's plan is always the highest plan.

When we are faithful, we not only demonstrate our trust in an Almighty God, but we also ignite the power to bring about the works of God. Where there is faith, God shows up and moves in mighty ways. Read through the Gospels and you will see countless miracles He performed for the faithful. Will we be found faithful when our circumstances are less than perfect?

Our faithfulness is proven by our actions, not just our words, and it should never rest on our circumstances, but on who God is. Faithfulness to Him has the power to change things and God will work according to our level of faith.

THE WORD :

1 Corinthians 15:58 (CEV)   *Matthew 9:29 (NIV)*
Colossians 2:6-7 (CEV)   *2 Timothy 4:7-8 (NLT)*
Isaiah 26:3 (CEV)   *James 2:14 (CEV)*
Jeremiah 17:7-8 (CEV)   *Mark 6:5-6 (CEV)*
Habakkuk 2:4b (MSG)

QUESTIONS :

1. What does God command His people concerning their faith?
2. What does God promise to the faithful?
3. What life circumstances have shaken my faith?
4. Is it possible that my lack of faith is preventing God from moving in my life?
5. Are there any actions I need to take to prove my faithfulness to the Lord?

nine

GUIDE

"PULL ME A LITTLE CLOSER, TAKE ME A LITTLE DEEPER,
I WANNA KNOW YOUR HEART, I WANNA KNOW YOUR HEART."

Steffany Frizzell Gretzinger

One of the biggest troubles for me as a single girl has always been what to do "next". Do I go on a date with this guy? Do I break up with this one? Should I push through and keep trying with him, because this is normal and relationships just take work? (All at separate times of course.)

As I look back now on over 12 years of dating (yikes!), I realize God never failed to tell me what to do. It wasn't always immediate and it wasn't always so clear at first, but He was ALWAYS faithful to guide me. And once I was obedient He always gave me a peace and assurance that I had done the right thing. But here's the thing, the question was never IF the Lord would guide me through these decisions, it was whether or not I was going to be close enough to Him to know His will.

I tend to overthink things and relationship stuff was no different. Anytime I started to stress out about what I was supposed to be doing, I had to remind myself to slow down and look to the Lord. It's so simple. Once I remembered that I had one thing to do- abide in Him - I felt overwhelming peace, knowing that He would not let me falter.

Stop trying to figure things out. Stop trying to connect the dots. Stop trying to rationalize your situation based on others' experiences. It will only make you crazy... I know, because it's what I used to do. Drawing close to the Father should be your only aim, especially in those moments. And you can trust that as you draw closer to Him, everything will fall into place.

As a Christian, you already have everything you need to live a life pleasing to the Lord. We have the Holy Spirit as our guide. Our job is to listen and obey. The more responsive we are to each prompting of the Spirit, the clearer it becomes. If you are actively abiding in the Lord, your heart will continually be molded to His heart.

"Take delight in the Lord, and he will give you the desires of your heart." Psalms 37:4

I bet you knew this verse was going to be in here. This is like the official creed of singles everywhere. But unfortunately a lot of women grasp tighter to this verse than any in the Bible. We have taken it to mean that if we delight in the Lord and do what He says, then He will give us our heart's desire, which for most is a husband. But what if, instead of this exchange, it means that as we spend our time delighting in the Lord, He puts His desires into our heart, and we begin to want the things that He wants and more naturally choose the way of the Lord?

I have done it both ways. I have tried to force myself to want the things of the Lord and then I have been so close to God that my heart began to crave the things He craves. Without a doubt the latter has always been the better way.

God will be my guide. We need only be close enough to Him to know His heart and where He wants us to go.

THE WORD :

Isaiah 58:11 (CEV)   *John 14:26 (CEV)*
Psalm 32:8 (NIV)   *John 16:13 (NIV)*
Isaiah 28:23-26,29 (NIV)   *Numbers 9:15-23 (CEV)*
Psalm 143:10 (ESV)

QUESTIONS :

1. What does God promise to those who seek guidance?
2. When God used a cloud to guide the Israelites, how many steps ahead did He show them? How much notice did they receive? How close were they to the cloud?
3. As a believer, I can have confidence that the Holy Spirit is helping me to understand the things of God, so what stops me from looking to the Lord for instruction? Do I have any doubts? Is there anything else I'm looking to?
4. What situations in my life do I need the Lord's guidance in?

ten

OBEY

"BEING A CHRISTIAN IS LESS ABOUT CAUTIOUSLY AVOIDING SIN,
THAN ABOUT COURAGEOUSLY & ACTIVELY DOING GOD'S WILL."

Dietrich Bonhoeffer

To obey is to submit to the command of another and coming from God, we know the command will always be for our own good. As Christians, there are 2 areas that require our obedience: The first is God's laws that are laid out for us in the Bible. They are black and white (with some grey areas that we tend to argue about), and we can easily know how He desires for us to live our lives. That is "easily know"...not easily do. The second area is what we just talked about in the last section. We are to obey the leading of the Holy Spirit in specific matters. This one requires much more intention and consistent reliance on the Holy Spirit to hear from Him as He speaks.

I have struggled with both of these. Being born and raised in the church and going to private school most of my life, I know the rules on dating. I am the one who, like Bonhoeffer said above, has spent years trying to cautiously avoid sin, instead of wholeheartedly pursuing the will of God. Which it turns out actually resulted in me falling into the same sin I was trying to avoid. It just doesn't work.

Once I began pursuing the Lord's heart and ultimately seeking His will for my life, these sins become less enticing. He replaced my fleshly desires with His righteous ones. I also found that these sins were hindrances to my intimacy and communication with God, so the closer I become with the Lord the more costly it was to my relationship with Him. When I am in the middle of His will, close to Him and being used by Him, it makes the sins I used to try, with so much energy to avoid, become much less desirable. There becomes a higher purpose in my life, and all other desires pale in comparison and the cost to my intimacy with Him is not worth it.

In regard to listening to the guidance of the Lord, over the years, there have been times that I was obedient, disobedient, and slowly obedient... which may as well be considered disobedient. I remember Him one time specifically telling me to end a relationship and I didn't. I eventually did... a year later. Even though I obeyed, because it was slow there were still consequences to my sin. But I did find that my obedience to His leading became quicker and quicker, as I grew in spiritual maturity and in recognizing God's voice.

One thing that we can be sure of is, like faith, those who can be trusted in small matters can be trusted in larger matters. I heard a speaker once talk about silence and not hearing from God, and she asked, "What was the last thing God told you to do? Did you do it?" We all want to hear from God, but what did we do with the last thing we heard? Did we brush it off and ask for another word??

Remember that disobedience blocks the pathway for fellowship and communion with God. Love the Lord, by keeping His commands and you will enjoy great intimacy and communion with the Father.

Our obedience to the Lord's commands and His leadings exemplifies our love for Him and our trust in His plan. The Lord will bless the obedient and His love will abide in them.

THE WORD :

John 14:15 (NLT)
Luke 11:28 (CEV)
Jeremiah 7:23 (ESV)
Psalm 97:11-12 (CEV)

Isaiah 30:1-3 (ESV)
Hebrews 3:7-11, 18 (ESV)
Galatians 6:7-8 (CEV)

QUESTIONS :

1. What does God promise to the obedient? And to the disobedient?
2. What commands do I struggle the most to obey?
3. What did I do with the last thing the Lord told me to do?
4. Is there any call that I have not been obedient to?

eleven

HOPE

"ONLY WHEN FALSE HOPE IS ABANDONED WILL MY
STRANGE, BUT TRUE HOPE BE EMBRACED."

66 Love Letters (Habbakuk)

One of the things that I have loved most about singleness is that it has stripped me of false hope. It would be easy to put my confidence for a future in a cute boyfriend, but without it I was pushed to search for true hope.

A great example of steady hope in the Bible is Joseph. At a very young age, he was shown a few dreams that gave him a vision for what God had for his future. Throughout his life he experienced many ups and downs and just when you'd think he was about to reach the promise, he was knocked back down again. I don't think anyone would have blamed Joseph if he gave up or second guessed himself thinking, "Maybe that's not what God meant" or "Maybe I screwed up along the way and it will never happen." But Joseph didn't do any of that. He was confident in God's plan and never lost hope. He relied on the promise and did not let his circumstances discourage him.

At times I have felt that maybe I veered off the path somewhere along the journey and that, through disobedience, I screwed up my chances of a husband in the future. How silly it was to think that the Lord is not more powerful than my choices. He is almighty and proves time and time again that He can use us even through all our missteps in life. Sometimes we may find ourselves in places and wonder how it could all end well. For Joseph it was jail... twice. But luckily for him and for us, that is not the end of the story.

During one of my break-ups, I remember in a moment of great clarity thinking, "As much as I care about this guy, I will love my future husband even more and he will be an even better match for me!" The idea was mind boggling to me. At the time I didn't understand how anyone could possibly be better. (I would love to go to teenage Natalie and show her a tidbit of the future. She would surely giggle.) But it was such a hopeful thing to think about. This was not the end of the story.

All of a sudden, hope found me. The endless possibilities and the fact that my future was still a blank canvas was so exciting to me! I learned then that such is the same with all of life! Everything I believe to be good and the things I want from life are nothing compared to the promises the Lord has for me and for my future. As small as our minds are compared to God's, there is no way we could come up with all the good that He has in store for us. If we asked Him for every blessing known to man we still could never come close to what He has planned.

As God is looking down on us, it must be like watching children try to fit a square into a circle. We try to force things that don't fit and aren't for our best, but we honestly have no clue what is ultimately good for us. All the while, we have a God in heaven who DOES know what is best and is piecing together a beautiful, intricate, and perfect puzzle for us.

It's like the old country song goes (By the way, I am a city girl at heart. Not sure how this slipped in.) "some of God's greatest gifts are unanswered prayers." Thank God that He sees so much more than we see and that He redeems us when we try to take over and get in the way!

We can be hopeful for a future that was designed by a God whose thoughts are so much higher than our thoughts. We can trust that His promises will be fulfilled and that He can redeem our missteps for His glory.

THE WORD :

Psalm 27:13 (NIV)
1 Corinthians 2:9 (CEV)
Isaiah 55:9 (NLT)
Ephesians 3:20 (NIV)

Proverbs 19:21 (ESV)
Job 42:2 (ESV)
Psalm 138:8 (ESV)
Ephesians 1:18-20 (NIV)

QUESTIONS :

1. What reasons do we have to hope in the Lord?
2. If I were to make a plan for my future, what would it be?
3. Is it possible that God has a better plan for me?
4. How much assurance does it give me to know that God is more than able to redeem our mistakes and complete His good work?

twelve

HEAVENLY

"IF I FOUND IN MYSELF A DESIRE WHICH NO EXPERIENCE IN
THIS WORLD CAN SATISFY, THE MOST PROBABLE EXPLANATION
IS THAT I WAS MADE FOR ANOTHER WORLD."

C.S. Lewis

We just talked about our hope and promises being fulfilled, but the truth is that some of these promises we will actually never see come to fruition here on earth. But that is ok, because luckily this world is not all there is. One of the biggest life changers for me recently was my grasp of a heavenly perspective.

Sounds kind of like a downer, right?? After getting you pumped up about how hopeful we can be about our future and then say that that may not happen till heaven... kind of feels like the rug has been pulled out, huh? But I believe that once you truly understand the heavenly perspective, it WILL give you hope.

Realizing that the promises of God still had room to be fulfilled in heaven, gave me the freedom to relax and not stress, because this life was not all there was. It was almost as if my timetable got longer. I don't EXPECT for this life to be the fulfillment of every promise, so it isn't as big of a disappointment if it doesn't happen.

We are commanded throughout the Bible to consider heavenly things as more valuable than earthly things. Several times, while speaking to his disciples and the people, Jesus experiences frustration with their lack of understanding of what He is saying. When you dig a little deeper you can see that Jesus is on another wavelength of thought. When He speaks, He speaks of spiritual and heavenly matters. He says "I am that bread from heaven! Everyone who eats it will live forever" (John 6:51) and they question how He will give them His flesh to eat. He also says "Very truly I tell you, no one can see the kingdom of God unless they are born again" (John 3:3) and Nicodemus asks how he can enter his mother's womb again.

I wonder how often the Lord is speaking to me and I interpret things with an earth-filled mind. It's naturally how we think, so it's understandable, but it's also the reason why transforming our minds to think like Christ is so necessary.

Contemplating this eternal lens has made me re-think verses like Jeremiah 29:11, "For I know the plans I have for you," declares the Lord, "plans to prosper you and not to harm you, plans to give you hope and a future." Or Romans 8:28, "And we know that in all things God works for the good of those who love him, who have been called according to his purpose." Have I mistakenly interpreted those to mean that my circumstances on earth will be good or that I will prosper in what I do here by the world's standards? Instead of this thought, could the "good" be growing in holiness regardless of my circumstances? And could the "hope" and "future" be in reference to when we finally get to heaven?

I can't answer that, because His plans could be for you to prosper and have a pleasing life here on earth, but that's not what we should place all our hope in. We are to consider the things of heaven as more important than things of earth. When we really, really get that, then we should fear nothing on earth. Not even lifelong singleness.

We are made for heaven, not for earth, and we are commanded to value our eternal home more than anything temporary. A heavenly perspective frees us from the chains of this world.

THE WORD :

2 Corinthians 4:18 (NIV) *Philippians 3:20a (NIV)*
Colossians 3:1-3 (NIV) *2 Corinthians 5:1-10 (NIV)*
Ecclesiastes 3:11 (NIV) *Romans 8:18-21 (MSG)*
Matthew 6:19-21 (ESV)

QUESTIONS :

1. What does the Lord command us concerning heaven?
2. How do heaven and earth compare to each other?
3. How might a heavenly perspective change the way I go through life?

thirteen

GREATER

Catherine Booth

How often do we take a step back from situations in life, forget about how they are affecting us, and look to see how they are affecting the world? As I started to grasp the idea of cultivating a life based on a heavenly perspective, it became increasingly clear to me that my life on earth was to serve a greater good than just living a God-honoring life in my little family. My life had a bigger purpose to serve the world and be a part of God's plan for the redemption of His people.

Throughout the Bible you will find stories of individuals who were called to serve the world with their life and it ultimately meant an uncomfortable and sometimes miserable life for most or all of their days. Joseph, Ezekial, Job, Nehemiah, Paul. They didn't feel entitled to a certain standard of life, they were just obedient to God's call. Their obedience not only blessed them (maybe on earth, but definitely in heaven), but it blessed the world.

At a women's retreat last year, our speaker taught on barrenness, using Hannah from the Bible, who became Samuel's mother, as our example. I immediately connected with the topic. As a single woman, I felt spiritually barren and I was excited to hear some compassionate words on the subject. Boy was I wrong. She didn't coddle me... she challenged me! She told of how Hannah spent years praying for a son. Then she said the phrase that I will never forget. She said "Hannah was praying for a son, but God needed a prophet." The world at that time, NEEDED a prophet, never mind want Hannah wanted. But Hannah faithfully accepted this call! I want to be like that. I want to live life with open hands to whatever the Lord asks me to do, for the betterment of His kingdom.

We talked earlier about God's intricate plan for His people, and how it is a privilege for us to participate in it. As Christians, we are left on earth to minister to His people - to love them, serve them, and ultimately bring them into His presence. If our purpose as Christians was merely to enjoy life and worship the Lord, then we could do that in heaven.

A single girl friend of mine and I were talking about this topic. I asked her about the possibility that maybe what the world needed at that moment was for her to be single. She is doing AMAZING things for His kingdom and her ability to be able to travel and have a singular focus is part of the reason she has been able to be used by God in so many areas.

I've often joked before with my single friends that if we were single then there HAD to be a big God reason, because we were such awesome catches! It was silly, sure, but there is some truth to that and I hope you feel the same way. If you are single right now, there is a reason. Maybe it's for some of the reasons we talked about earlier, like a need for dependence on the Lord or disobedience, but maybe, just maybe it could be for something else. Maybe He has a bigger and grander call for your life in service to the world!

Our life is not our own and we should offer it in service to something greater -
God's redemption of the world.

THE WORD :

Genesis 12:1-3 (NLT)   John 6:38 (NIV)
Acts 20:24 (NIV)   Ephesians 2:10 (NIV)
1 Corinthians 10:23-24 (NIV)   Matthew 5:16 (CEV)
1 Corinthians 12:7 (NIV)   Ecclesiastes 2:1 (NIV)

QUESTIONS :

1. What did Abram sacrifice to follow God? Who was blessed because of it?
2. What am I on this earth for?
3. How would my life look different if I was living for others rather than myself?

fourteen

IDOL

"ANYTIME WITH PRIORITIZED ENERGY I DO ANYTHING TO
FILL MY EMPTINESS OR TO PROTECT MYSELF FROM MORE
REJECTION, I AM SERVING THE WRONG KINGDOM."

Larry Crabb

In these modern times our pastors have done a pretty good job of teaching on the new "modern day" idols. We no longer struggle, like the Israelites did, with images or statues, (although I'm sure some people still do), but what we have done is prioritize things like money and success in our life above God, which in turn become idols. But I wonder how many of us realize that we have put the ideas of marriage and motherhood on a pedestal and set them up as idols in our own life.

An idol is ANYTHING we desire that distracts us from pursuing the Lord or pulls us away from the heart of God. It can be good things too, potential blessings that the Father wants to give us, but if they take up too much of our heart and thoughts, then they are squeezing God out.

Is it wrong to desire to be married? No
Is it wrong to pray for our future husband? Of course not.

We cross the line when the thing that we desire is at the forefront of our mind, when it consumes our thoughts and influences our actions more than the truth in God's word influences us.

A possible danger with being single for a long time can be that, as women, we can romanticize marriage and make up a picture in our mind of what we think it will be. After desiring and thinking about something for years, we can distort the reality of what marriage actually is and what it will do for us. It then becomes this larger than life goal that we pursue with more energy than anything else.

At that point, we not only set ourselves up for failure, but we are setting our potential spouses up for failure too. If we are not careful, we can actually trade the blessings of the Lord and all that He designed for marriage, for the distorted desires of our heart.

Give yourself a quick heartcheck. How big has the desire of marriage gotten in your life? How often do you think about it? And how much energy do you put into thinking about it, pursuing it, or talking about?

The idea of marriage can actually become an idol if we let it. Do not hold more tightly to your desire for marriage than your desire for the Lord.

THE WORD :

Romans 13:14 (NIV)　　　　*Isaiah 42:8 (CEV)*
Romans 1:25 (NLT)　　　　*James 4:4-5 (MSG)*
Jeremiah 2:13 (NIV)

QUESTIONS :

1. What is idolatry according to the Bible?
2. What am I trading in when I choose idols over the Lord?
3. Am I holding too tightly to the idea of marriage or motherhood?

fifteen

EQUIP

"WHAT YOU LEARNED IN THE PROCESS WILL
SERVE YOU IN THE PROMISE."

Jen Tringale

One of the huge benefits to singleness is the free time we have. Once I realized that this will most likely be the most free-time I will ever have, I became more intentional about what I was doing with my time. Now, I'll be honest, I can binge on Netflix like the best of us, but I have pushed myself to discover, learn, and pursue new things. Singleness for me has been the single most valuable time in my life in regards to my relationship with God and my own personal maturity. I feel so much more equipped than I did 10 years ago to handle whatever the future holds for me. I also feel confidant that God is not done with me yet and will keep teaching me as I keep my heart open to Him.

While working on this devotional, I looked back over journals and notes from the past 5 years. It revealed just how big God's picture is. He was equipping me for my present circumstances with lessons I learned years ago, before I even knew why.

This season of singleness can be an incredible time of equipping for what comes next. Maybe it's marriage. Maybe it's not. Maybe it's kids. Maybe it's not. I know for me, the last year I have felt more prepared for the future than ever before and it's all because of what God had taught me, throughout the past decade.

Jesus showed us the importance of being equipped in His own life. When He was tempted by the devil in the wilderness, He fought back with Scripture. It was truth that He had already received and stored up. This serves as a reminder that battles are usually won in advance. He was prepared against Satan's attacks and didn't have to search for the answers on the spot. Imagine being prepared like Jesus was for anything that came your way!

During this time of learning and equiping, we can also pray that God would give us a vision of what kind of woman we would be as a wife and mother. It seems as though we all have a future husband wishlist, so why not dream about what character traits we'd love to possess and pray for God to develop those in our lives. A lot, if not all of the things we have talked about and will talk about in this study can benefit you in a future marriage and motherhood, not just singleness.

And remember, we will never have it all figure out. Once you "get good" at one stage of life, you will be on to the next and have a whole new set of things to learn. So commit now to seeking the Lord and developing spiritual maturity all throughout life, so that you can be ready for every good work He has prepared for you to do.

Singleness can actually help prepare you for the promises of God, whether that is marriage, motherhood, or something completely different, if you let it. You can waste the time or you can invest the time.

THE WORD :

Psalm 1:1-3 (ESV)   *2 Timothy 2:15 (NLT)*
2 Timothy 3:16-17 (NLT)   *Proverbs 6:6-8 (ESV)*
Ephesians 4:11-16 (ESV)   *Luke 12:40 (CEV)*

QUESTIONS :

1. What does the Lord use to equip us?
2. Being prepared requires work! Am I actively searching for His wisdom and truth?
3. What lessons can I learn from singleness that could help me in marriage?
4. In motherhood?

sixteen

BITTER

"PEACE, JOY, CONTENTMENT, & FULFILLMENT ARE NOT DEPENDENT
ON CIRCUMSTANCES OR PEOPLE, BUT ON BEHOLDING GOD."

Darien B. Cooper

I hope that all we have talked about has opened your eyes to the many blessings that the Lord has in store for our single years, but I am not naïve enough to think that everyone who is reading this is happy about their status. I know that after years of waiting and praying and fighting the expectations of the world, bitterness can sneak in. We can begin to feel bitter toward those whose circumstances we would rather and we can even become bitter towards God for allowing it. I believe that the root cause of bitterness is when we leave our discontentedness unchecked for too long.

Contentment. You probably knew we would discuss being content about our status at some point. We have to, because it is a huge obstacle for many singles, but my hope is that when we focus on the truths that we have seen throughout this study and appreciate God's ultimate plan, that contentment will naturally follow. I came across this definition of content recently - "Rest in one's present state." I pray that we would learn to rest in our present state, as is, because of who our God is.

This topic, like many of the others, does not apply only to singlehood. It may just be that unexpected singleness is the first big life plan where things don't go exactly as you thought they would. The truth is, there will be situations ALL throughout life that we will have to decide to have peace in our situation. It happens when conceiving a baby doesn't happen as soon as you like, or marriage isn't exactly what you thought it would be. Learning to be content now will serve you throughout your lifetime.

"Guard your heart above all else, for it determines the course of your life."
Proverbs 4:23 (NLT)

The Bible tells us that the heart is where all life flows from, so it is important to guard against discontent and work to remove bitterness as soon as we see it taking root.

So what do you do if bitterness has already taken up space in your heart? First and foremost, I would recommend praying for God to change your heart about the subject, spending time abiding in the Lord's presence, and transforming your mind, by studying His word. It can seem cliché or like the Sunday school response to say "Jesus is the answer for everything!", but the truth is that He is the most powerful force of heart change that I've ever experienced and I know the same will be true for you if you only seek after Him. Next, I would encourage you to begin a gratitude list and intentionally look for things that you appreciate that the Lord HAS done in your life. Lastly, I'd tell you to pray for those that cause you the most bitterness and actively pursue to show them love.

Anything is possible with the Lord, so begin by believing that HE is capable of melting away even the strongest hold of bitterness in your life. Do your part and leave the heart change up to God.

Bitterness must be actively guarded against, by beholding the presence of the Lord, practicing contentment for our circumstance, guarding what comes into our heart, and not falling into the trap of comparison.

THE WORD :

Proverbs 15:15 (CEV)	Leviticus 19:18 (ESV)
1 Timothy 6:6-8 (NLT)	Hebrews 12:15 (NLT)
Psalm 50:23 (NLT)	Psalms 73:21-26 (NLT)

QUESTIONS :

1. What does the Bible say about contentment and thankfulness?
2. When do I feel the most discontent?
3. Does anyone in particular trigger my bitterness? How can I pray for them?
4. Have I allowed bitterness to take root?

seventeen

LAUGH

"SHE LAUGHS WITHOUT FEAR OF THE FUTURE."

Proverbs 31:25b

I love the imagery in the verse above of a woman who is so free from worry that she is laughing! Women tend be natural worriers, so to me this is a beautiful picture of what having Christ in our lives can do.

First things first, though, before we can laugh we must be free from constant worry in our hearts. It's so easy to convince ourselves that once we are married we won't worry so much and we will enjoy life a little more, but that is just wishful thinking. When we are married, we might worry about our relationship with our husband and when we have children we might worry about their every step from now till adulthood (and beyond). Worry has less to do with our situation and more to do with how we handle things that come our way. So, my hope is that we'd figure out how to deal with worry now, so whenever it comes upon us we can fight it.

There is a story in the gospels about Jesus and the disciples encountering a terrible storm, while traveling by boat. Frightened, the disciples woke Jesus who had fallen sleep. He got up, calmed the storm, then He asked "Why were you afraid? Don't you have any faith?" From this passage we learn a few things about worry. First, it tells us what we don't always like to admit, that worry shows a lack of faith. Next, it teaches us that sometimes Jesus purposely brings us into the very situations that worry us the most to show us His power and to test our faith. The first line of this passage says "Jesus said, 'Let's cross to the east side.'" It was Jesus' plan all along. He knew what would happen.

I love the words of this song that remind me of this story.
"Let go, my soul and trust in Him, the waves and wind still know his name."

I find such freedom in this thought. Our souls are weary and burdened by the things of this world, but He is calling us to let go of them, because we know that He is able. The fact that the waves and wind know His name tells me that even they are under His command. Nothing happens that He is not in ultimate control over. When we begin to trust that the Lord's plan for me, whatever it is, will be a good plan for His Kingdom, we can rest and then we can laugh.

I remember finally letting go of all the expectations I had and the "supposed to's" of life. It was then that I decided to embrace the single gal lifestyle, knowing that this was God's plan for the time and it was all in His hands. That is when I started to have fun with it! It took some time to break old habits and build new ones. There were some days when I would just have to tell myself "Come on Natalie, you have to fake it till you make it!" I found that sometimes I just had to DECIDE to laugh, before I actually FELT like laughing. But before long, I had created a habit of loving and enjoying the single life that was genuine and came naturally.

During this time, I came across the Message version of Ecclesiastes 11:10a and it just made me smile! "Live footloose & fancy free – You won't be young forever. Youth lasts about as long as smoke." The Bible encourages us to enjoy life and reminds us that our time here is brief. That's what my prayer is for all of you! I want to see single women dig so deep into their relationship with the Lord and learning His truth that they have no other option, but to laugh and begin loving life - even the single life!

Those who are close to the Lord and trust in His name do not worry about the future. They delight in Him and enjoy their position in life, wherever it may be.

THE WORD :

Philippians 4:6-7 (CEV)   *Ecclesiastes 5:18-20 (MSG)*
Luke 12:29-31 (CEV)   *Ecclesiastes 8:15 (NIV)*
Proverbs 20:24 (NLT)   *Psalm 33:21 (NLT)*

QUESTIONS :

1. What causes worry?
2. What causes joy?
3. What specifically am I anxious about this season of life?
4. What can I do to relax and spend more time enjoying and celebrating my time of singleness?

eighteen

SATISFIED

"NO LOVE OF THE NATURAL HEART IS SAFE UNLESS THE
HUMAN HEART HAS BEEN SATISFIED BY GOD FIRST."

Oswald Chambers

A common struggle of the single life is the feeling of incompleteness. It hurts to think about all the times that my actions told the Lord that He was not enough for me. I didn't see it like that at the time, but anytime my desire for a husband was too great, it was like I was saying that my relationship with the Lord was not satisfying me.

In Luke 10, Jesus visits the house of Mary & Martha. Martha is busy preparing the house and attending to the logistics and Mary just sits at Jesus' feet. When Martha complains to Him that she is not helping, Jesus responds, "Martha, Martha! You are worried and upset about so many things, but only one thing is necessary. Mary has chosen what is best, and it will not be taken away from her."

Only one thing is necessary. I love that! Jesus is telling us that we are not lacking ANYTHING. If we have this "one thing" we are all set! We can be complete and we can be completely satisfied.

The Lord is enough to satisfy all my needs and desires and it is my job to start living like it. The Bible says we have been made "complete through your union with Christ," (Colossians 2:10 NLT). We've got to stop seeing ourselves as partial people until we are a couple. It can be difficult because we live in a world of twosomes, but we are assured by God that because of our union with Jesus we are complete in Him.

I can honestly say that I'm grateful for the years of singleness that pushed me to seek Him to complete me. With Him, we experience the most complete and perfect love imaginable. If it wasn't for this time alone, I may have filled the void with a man, and never truly found satisfaction in Him alone for all my needs. Even though we try, we will never be satisfied with any person until we are satisfied first by God. On top of that, when we allow Him to fulfill our deepest needs and desires it frees those around us, including a future husband, to love us like an imperfect person will. We can remove unrealistic pressures for them to fill the hole in our heart that only our God can.

I'll leave you with this quote ...
"God is most glorified in us when we are most satisfied in Him." – John Piper

With all the things that we try to do to please God, we know that it is our love and delight in Him alone that He most desires.

The Lord alone will satisfy all of our needs. We are made complete in Him, not lacking in anything.

THE WORD :

Psalms 62:1-2, 5 (ESV)
Psalms 73:25-26 (NIV)
Psalm 107:9 (ESV)
2 Peter 1:3 (CEV)

Psalms 145:15-16 (CEV)
2 Corinthians 9:8 (NLT)
Isaiah 55:1-2 (NIV)
Luke 10:38-42 (CEV)

QUESTIONS :

1. What does the Bible say will be my satisfaction?
2. What am I to do with what I receive?
3. What else am I currently looking for to satisfy me?
4. How might knowing I'm complete and being satisfied by God help me in future relationships?

nineteen

RECEIVE

"LET HIM WHO IS ABLE TO RECEIVE THIS RECEIVE IT."

Matthew 19:12b

Out of all the books I have read and sermons I've heard on singleness, I have only heard the following passage preached about one time. I understand that it's not very popular and the word "eunuch" probably makes people uncomfortable, but it's in God's Word and from Jesus' lips so we must pay attention to it.

While talking about divorce, the disciples commented that if this was a possible outcome of marriage, then it was better not to marry at all. And this was Jesus' reply...
"Only those people who have been given the gift of staying single can accept this teaching. Some people are unable to marry because of birth defects or because of what someone has done to their bodies. Others stay single for the sake of the kingdom of heaven. Anyone who can accept this teaching should do so." Matthew 19:11-12

His response has taught me 3 things about singleness:
1. It is a **gift**. Some people are gifted with singleness. If you are one of those people He will help you (see NLT version).
2. It is **hard**. Even some who are called to it will not be able to accept it.
3. It is **better** for the kingdom. Jesus is telling those who have been called to it to receive and accept singleness for His kingdom's sake.

A **GIFT**. In talking with the wisest single gal I know (I pray that each of you find a mentor like her to walk with you through singleness!), we both ended up saying that we sometimes felt special, because God had called us to singleness, even if only for a season. If you are called by the Lord to remain single for His kingdom, for any length of time, I hope you feel special that He has chosen you for this gift too. It is such a unique calling and if He calls you to it, He will help you through it.

HARD. Just because we are called to it doesn't make it easy. Something can be good and purposeful, but still hard. Marriage is the same, it is a good gift, but it doesn't mean

121

that it is easy. You wouldn't expect for a marriage to be easy, so why do we expect that a call to singlehood means that we will never struggle through it?

BETTER. Jesus and Paul said that singleness was the "better way". This is not to diminish the calling of marriage or motherhood, because God uses them to serve purposes for His plan also. But as far as time and freedom, you are able to do MORE through seasons of singleness.

I've heard people, too many times, take Paul's stance on singleness as radical and biased, because it does not fit in well with the American culture. But the truth is, many Biblical truths don't fit with American culture. This is why it is so important to value the things of heaven as more important and to transform our thinking to that of the mind of Christ.

I believe that this is a big reason why God has called me to write this devotional. There are women who have been called to remain single for the Gospel and haven't received it yet. We must embrace the privilege of singleness for the sake of Christ, become effective at our calling, and determine to receive whatever He has called us to do.

The Lord calls some to singleness, because it is better for His kingdom. If we are called and are able to receive this truth, we should, and we will be blessed by it.

THE WORD :

Isaiah 56:3b-5 (NLT)   *1 Corinthians 7:25-40 (CEV)*
1 Corinthians 7:7-9 (NLT)   *Matthew 19:10-12 (CEV)*

QUESTIONS :

1. What does God promise to those who remain single (eunuchs)?
2. Do I believe that singleness is a gift? Is the better thing?
3. I am ABLE to do more as a single for His Kingdom, but am I doing more?
4. Is the Lord calling me to singleness, for any period of time? If so, am I willing to receive this call?

twenty

SURRENDER

"EVERYTHING IS SAFE WHICH WE COMMIT TO HIM,
AND NOTHING IS REALLY SAFE WHICH IS NOT."

A.W. Tozer

I remember praying to God and offering up my future to Him about whether I would eventually be married. With my hands physically out, I surrendered it all to Him and it was scary! I thought I had done this years before, but it wasn't with the true surrender that I felt this time. In the past, I worried that my act of surrender would surely mean that I would be single for life. Almost as if God was just looking for someone naive enough to hand it over, that He could take up on their offer, cause no one else was willing to do it.

In the past, what I secretly hoped for was an Abraham and Isaac story. I hoped that the second I surrendered it, he would give it right back and I would meet my husband, like all He wanted was to see if I was willing to surrender it to Him. Abraham was asked to sacrifice the son that for years he had prayed for, and right when he was about to kill him and complete the sacrifice, an angel stopped him and said "Don't lay a hand on the boy! Do not hurt him in any way, for now I know that you truly fear God. You have not withheld from me even your son, your only son." Yes, that was the story of surrender I wanted, the ending I was hoping for.

At that point, I hadn't heard the story about Hannah who would become Samuel's mother. Hannah, like Abraham, also prayed for a child for years and years. She promised that if the Lord blessed her with a son that she would give him back to God and that he would serve the church. When Samuel was at the proper age, she fulfilled her promise and surrendered him to Eli's care to become a priest. He wasn't returned back to her as Isaac had been to Abraham, but the story doesn't end there. Hannah was blessed for her surrender and faithfulness. She not only had 5 more children, but as the mother of Samuel, who eventually anointed David king, she had a part in the legacy of the line of Jesus Christ.

It took a while, but I did finally realize what true surrender looked like. I wasn't going to hope for any situation that happened to anyone else, but I would truly only hope for God to use me as He saw fit and to give me what He felt was best for my life. A friend once told me that every few months she intentionally prays and gives her singleness to God. Ever since she told me this I started praying "Lord, I place this situation in your hands." I'd lift my hands as if to physically give it to God. I also began doing this after I started dating someone, as a reminder that although God gave me this blessing, it would always be in my best interest to entrust it back to the Creator.

He calls ALL of us to give up our lives and put them in His hands. Every part of our life, for all the years of our life. We will not know if God will keep what we offer up to Him or if He will give it back. What we do know is that we can never out give God. Whatever He gives back will be more than we ever imagined. Surrender is not actually about us "giving up" anything. The Lord already has something in mind, but by surrender He allows us to participate in His great plan. We are trading our small plans for His grand plans.

We will never truly find life until we offer all that we are to all that He is. We will have opportunities in every stage of life to trade our ways for God's ways, and participate in His grand design. Once we really get to know our Creator we won't be able to surrender to Him fast enough.

THE WORD :

Luke 9:23-27 (CEV)   *John 12:24-25 (NIV)*
Luke 14:25-33 (CEV)   *Romans 12:1 (MSG)*
John 6:38 (NIV)   *Matthew 26:39 (NLT)*

QUESTIONS :

1. What does God promise to those who surrender to Him?
2. Who is our greatest example of surrender? What was His response to His call?
3. What is God calling me to surrender?
4. Do I trust that God is worthy of my surrender?

twenty-one

WHOLEHEARTEDLY

"WITH MY WHOLE HEART, FOR MY WHOLE LIFE."

Unknown

Over and over again in the Bible, God commands us to love with our whole heart. This must mean that there are too many of us who are giving Him only parts of our heart and lives. On Pinterest, you have probably seen the quote "with my whole heart, for my whole life." It is plastered all over newlywed things. Pillows, posters, invitations, you name it. It made me wonder how we can make this promise to an imperfect man, but still cannot commit fully to our Creator.

Our Creator is the only one worthy of our whole heart. He continually proves His love and faithfulness to us and will never let us down. Jesus paid the ultimate price by dying on the cross for our sins.

Like I mentioned earlier, soon after entering into a relationship, I actually began to miss singlehood! I wrote in my journal about how much I longed for the intimate time that I had with the Lord and the connection I experienced with Him. I quickly realized that I was missing my single years, because I hadn't figured out how to pursue the Lord wholeheartedly while in a relationship.

Wholeheartedness is not something just for singles. It's not something you forgo once you are married. But it is an easier lesson to learn as a single person, while your whole heart is unencumbered. So learn it now. Make it a habit. Build a foundation of loving the Lord with your whole heart for your whole life. And when the time comes, you will figure out how to take part in a relationship, while still pursing the Lord wholeheartedly.

The Lord demands and deserves our pursuit of Him wholeheartedly.
All we have to gain from this is everything.

THE WORD :

Psalm 9:1 (ESV)
Psalm 138:1 (CEV)
Psalm 119 (NIV)
Revelation 3:15-16 (CEV)
Jeremiah 24:7 (NLT)
Dueteronomy 6:4-9 (NLT)

Joshua 24:14 (NLT)
Psalm 86:12 (NLT)
Matthew 10:37-38 (NIV)
Dueteronomy 10:12-13 (NIV)
Jeremiah 29:13 (NLT)

QUESTIONS :

1. What does the Lord command that we are to do wholeheartedly?
2. What does God promise to those who pursue Him wholeheartedly?
3. And those who don't?
4. What is keeping you from pursuing the Lord wholeheartedly?
5. What would it look like to pursue Him with your whole heart?

Life Application

LET'S APPLY
THESE
TRUTHS

What topics did I find the most challenging in this study? Why?

_____

_____

_____

_____

_____

_____

_____

_____

_____

_____

What was the most surprising truth? Why?

_____

_____

_____

_____

_____

_____

_____

_____

_____

_____

_____

How is what I learned going to effect my life?

_____

_____

_____

_____

_____

_____

_____

_____

_____

_____

_____

What do I need to change to start living based on God's truths and promises?

_____

_____

_____

_____

_____

_____

_____

_____

_____

_____

_____

What specifically is God calling me to that I need to take action on?

My Story

THE GIRL
BEHIND
THE STUDY

Do you know anyone whose life was changed by a board game?
Now you do.

One night on our family beach trip, we decided to play monopoly. Or I should say my mom decided we would play. We were not five minutes into the game and my twin sister, Val, is killing it! She is buying up everything and with every roll she's hitting a double or the lottery. Or atleast it seemed like that to me. On top of that her super competitive side started coming out and she was singing and dancing and basically trying anything to annoy me... but I digress.

I do not know what came over me, but all of a sudden I became overcome with jealousy. She had a wonderful husband and the most perfect child you have ever met, and they had all just moved into the cutest little bungalow in our family's neighborhood development. She's known her purpose for years, has a thriving company with Val Marie Paper, and just that day had been asked to contribute on a book with lots of prestigious women. AND NOW SHE'S WINNING MONOPOLY TOO?!?!

I don't have those moments to often, but this time it came with avengeance. In my mind, Val beating me at monopoly just reiterated the lie that Val was beating me at life. Then came the pouting... if she was acting like a sore winner then I was definitely acting like a sore loser. I walked off for a minute to go the bathroom (aka pout in private) and when I came back I had a stack of money and a few new properties sitting in front of me. Turns out my risk-taking brother-in-law lost it all to me on the one property I owned... a railroad.

I couldn't believe it! I was still in this thing! I decided right then not to give up and I made a plan to buy all the railroads. (I'm pretty sure I guilted my brother into trading me his with "Val has everything, just like real life!" and a tear. He hated her dancing even more than I did though, so he quickly obliged.) I purchased all the railroads and a few other properties and would you believe it... I actually won!

To go from such a hopeless beginning to turning it around and winning it all, I just couldn't believe it. And honestly it gave me way more confidence than winning any board game should, but it actually taught me something.

I had felt that I was behind the curve in life, like some of you may feel. Having a twin sister has sometimes felt like a barometer for life. She has had the same amount of years, same upbringing, and a lot of the same experiences as me, so how was she so much further along? But what I have learned is that the Lord is going to take people at different paces to different places, so there is really no use comparing.

The next morning, Val came down to meet me while I was reading by the pool. With excitement in her voice she bursts out "I know what you're supposed to do!" (A little back story, I had been praying for YEARS for God to show me His purpose for my life. I've had a desire to be used by Him in a big way and seemed like I had been searching for His call for forever). So she continues "You need to write a devotional for singles!" and I just said "I need to write a devotional for singles." Immediately, just like that, I knew that God was calling me to do this.

About two weeks later, I was headed out of town for a fun single girl's night with a close friend of mine. On my drive over, I was praying and listening to some worship music when I really felt the

Lord speak to me. He had already spoken to me at the retreat "You are praying for a husband, but I need a prophet," like He had spoken to Hannah about her prayers for a son. I wondered if He meant that my future husband was going to be special in some way or what. I had no idea what it meant, but I knew without a doubt that He had given me that word. On this night, while listening to my anthem "Overwhelmed", He told me "You are praying for a husband, but I need a prophet... and YOU are that prophet." It was in that moment that He called me to be a prophet. He was calling me to speak His words to His people (specifically single gals!) through this devotional. I was overwhelmed with emotion and gratefulness at the revelation and it felt like the best day ever!

That night I met a guy. It was completely unexpected and I honestly wasn't looking for it, but sparks flew. A few weeks later, we had the best first date ever and started dating very soon after. We were in love! I very quickly became distracted and put this devotional idea aside. Until a few months later, when I felt the Lord telling me... "I asked you to do something. You have prayed for years to know what it was you were called to do for my kingdom and I told you something I needed. You haven't done it yet. Take a break from this relationship, so that you can complete this. And trust me." Of course it didn't sound that clear at first. It was more like weeks of me questioning how my heart could possibly be thinking about taking a step back from the most "perfect for me" guy I have ever met. And weeks of me causing fights, because I was so confused. And weeks of me feeling like something was wrong with me or that I was sabotaging this?!? You get the picture!

That's when I stopped and remembered what the Lord had proven true to me all along through my singleness. He would guide me – all I needed was to stay close to Him. As I drew closer, He gave me complete confidence that I could trust Him with this relationship. The Lord was giving me another opportunity to surrender my relationship status to Him for the benefit of His kingdom. He showed me in a very obvious way that only He can do, that He was in control and that if we are to be married one day, this little step back would not only not split us, but that it would actually make us stronger. So did I get my happily ever after with Mr. Wonderful???

Well at the time I first published the devotional this was my answer...
"I can't tell you how that story ends, because I don't know yet! It's still being unfolded. All I know is that I will have a happily ever after, because I know who holds it. Regardless of my relationship status, the Lord has proven to me that He is all I need and that He is worthy of my whole heart."

Unfolding it was! Three years later, I can share that I am now married to Mr. Wonderful - Josh Lewis, as he's known to the rest of the world! I'm finding myself daily learning what it means to be a wife who still pursues the Lord wholeheartedly and looking back on my single season with the sweetest of memories :).

Praying for you always, that you will answer His call and enjoy the great adventure that is singleness!   <3 Natalie

Scripture Verses

FOR WHEN YOU'RE ON THE GO

DAY #1 : THE MIND

Romans 12:2 (ESV)
"Do not be conformed to this world, but be transformed by the renewal of your mind, that by testing you may discern what is the will of God, what is good and acceptable and perfect."

2 Corinthians 10:5 (NLT)
"We destroy every proud obstacle that keeps people from knowing God. We capture their rebellious thoughts and teach them to obey Christ."

Romans 8:6 (NIV)
"The mind governed by the flesh is death, but the mind governed by the spirit is life and peace."

Philippians 4:8 (CEV)
"Finally, my friends, keep your minds on whatever is true, pure, right, holy, friendly, and proper. Don't ever stop thinking about what is truly worthwhile and worthy of praise."

1 Corinthians 2:12 (NLT)
"And we have received God's Spirit (not the world's spirit), so we can know the wonderful things God has freely given us."

Matthew 16:21-23 (CEV)
"From then on, Jesus began telling his disciples what would happen to him. He said, "I must go to Jerusalem. There the nation's leaders, the chief priests, and the teachers of the Law of Moses will make me suffer terribly. I will be killed, but three days later I will rise to life." Peter took Jesus aside and told him to stop talking like that. He said, "God would never let this happen to you, Lord!" Jesus turned to Peter and said, "Satan, g0et away from me! You're in my way because you think like everyone else and not like God."

DAY #2 : WORLDLY

1 Samuel 16:7 (NIV)
"But the Lord said to Samuel, "Do not consider his appearance or his height, for I have rejected him. The Lord does not look at the things people look at. People look at the outward appearance, but the Lord looks at the heart."

Galatians 1:10 (NIV)
"Am I now trying to win the approval of human beings, or of God? Or am I trying to please people? If I were trying to please people, I would not be a servant of Christ."

2 Corinthians 10:3 (CEV)
"We live in this world, but we don't act like its people."

1 John 2:15-17 (CEV)
"Don't love the world or anything that belongs to the world. If you love the world, you cannot love the Father. Our foolish pride comes from this world, and so do our selfish desires and our desire to have everything we see. None of this comes from the Father. The world and the desires it causes are disappearing. But if we obey God, we will live forever."

1 John 5:4,18 (ESV)
"For everyone who has been born of God overcomes the world. And this is the victory that has overcome the world – our faith."
"We know that we are from God, and the whole world lies in the power of the evil one."

Luke 14:15-24 (NIV)
"When one of those at the table with him heard this, he said to Jesus, 'Blessed is the one who will eat at the feast in the kingdom of God." Jesus replied: "A certain man was preparing a great banquet and invited many guests. At the time of the banquet he sent his servant to tell those who had been invited, 'Come, for everything is now ready.' But they all alike began to make excuses. The first said, 'I have just bought a field, and I must go and see it. Please excuse me.' Another said, 'I have just bought five yoke of oxen, and I'm on my way to try them out. Please excuse me.' Still another said, 'I just got married, so I can't come.' The servant came back and reported this to his master. Then the owner of the house became angry and ordered his servant, 'Go out quickly into the streets and alleys of the town and bring in the poor, the crippled, the blind and the lame.' 'Sir,' the servant said, 'what you ordered has been done, but there is still room.' "Then the master told his servant, 'Go out to the roads and country lanes and compel them to come in, so that my house will be full. I tell you, not one of those who were invited will get a taste of my banquet.'"

Hebrews 12:1 (NIV)
"Let us throw off everything that hinders."

DAY #3 : SEASONS

Ecclesiastes 3:1 (CEV)
"Everything on earth has its own time and its own season."

1 Thessalonians 5:18 (NIV)
"Give thanks in all circumstances; for this is God's will for you in Christ Jesus."

James 4:13-15 (NIV)
"Now listen, you who say 'Today or tomorrow we will go to this or that city, spend a year there, carry on business and make money.'"

2 Timothy 4:2a (NIV)
"preach the word; be prepared in season and out of season;"

DAY #4 : DEPENDENCE

Matt 5:3 (MSG)
"Your blessed when you're at the end of you rope. With less of you there is more of God and his rule."

Colossians 2:6-7 (NLT)
"And now, just as you accepted Christ Jesus as your Lord, you must continue to follow him. Let our roots grow down into him, and let you lives be built on him. Then your faith will grow strong in the truth you were taught, and you will overflow with thankfulness."

Psalm 62:5-6 (CEV)
"Only God gives inward peace, and I depend on him. God alone is the mighty rock that keeps me safe, and he is the fortress where I feel secure."

Exodus 4:10-12 (CEV)
"Moses replied, 'I have never been a good speaker. I wasn't one before you spoke to me, and I'm not one now. I am slow speaking, and I can never think of what to say.' But the Lord answered, 'Who makes people able to speak or makes them deaf or unable to speak? Who gives them sight or makes them blind? Don't you know that I am the one who does these things? Now go! When you speak, I will be with you and give you the words to say.' "

Jeremiah 17:5-8 (NIV)
"This is what the Lord says: "Cursed is the one who trusts in man, who draws strength from mere flesh and whose heart turns away from the Lord. That person will be like a bush in the wastelands; they will not see prosperity when it comes. They will dwell in the parched places of the desert, in a salt land where no one lives. "But blessed is the one who trusts in the Lord, whose confidence is in him. They will be like a tree planted by the water that sends out its roots by the stream. It does not fear when heat comes; its leaves are always green. It has no worries in a year of drought and never fails to bear fruit."

2 Corinthians 12:8-10 (NLT)
"Three different times I begged the Lord to take it away. Each time he said, "My grace is all you need. My power works best in weakness.' So now I am glad to boast about my weaknesses, so that the power of Christ can work through me. That's why I take pleasure in my weaknesses, and in the insults, hardships, persecutions, and troubles that I suffer for Christ. For when I am weak, then I am strong."

DAY #5 : THE GIFT GIVER

1 Chronicles 16:10-11 (NIV)
"Glory in his holy name; let the hearts of those who seek the Lord rejoice! Seek the Lord and his strength; seek his presence continually!"

Psalm 119:37 (CEV)
"Take away my foolish desires, and let me find life by walking with you."

James 4:8a (NLT)
"Come close to God and He will come close to you."

Psalm 27:4 (MSG)
"I'm asking God for one thing, only one thing; to live with him in his house my whole life long. I'll contemplate his beauty; I'll study at his feet."

Psalm 73:28 (NLT)
"But as for me, how good it is to be near God! I have made the Sovereign Lord my shelter, and I will tell everyone about the wonderful things you do."

Psalms 16 (CEV)
"Protect me, Lord God! I run to you for safety, and I have said, "Only you are my Lord! Every good thing I have is a gift from you." Your people are wonderful, and they make me happy, but worshipers of other gods will have much sorrow. I refuse to offer sacrifices of blood to those gods or worship in their name. You, Lord, are all I want! You are my choice, and you keep me safe. You make my life pleasant, and my future is bright. I praise you, Lord, for being my guide. Even in the darkest night, your teachings fill my mind. I will always look to you, as you stand beside me and protect me from fear. With all my heart, I will celebrate, and I can safely rest. I am your chosen one. You won't leave me in the grave or let my body decay. You have shown me the path to life, and you make me glad by being near to me. Sitting at your right side, I will always be joyful."

DAY #6 : CELEBRATE

Proverbs 15:30 (ESV)
"The light of the eyes rejoices the heart, and good news refreshes the bones."

Proverbs 118: 24 (CEV)
"This day belongs to the Lord! Let's celebrate and be glad today!"

Philippians 2:3-4 (CEV)
"Now make me completely happy! Live in harmony by showing love for each other. Be united in what you think, as if you were only one person. Don't be jealous or proud, but be humble and consider others more important than yourselves."

Romans 12:15 (NIV)
"Rejoice with those who rejoice."

Galatians 5:14 (ESV)
"For the whole law is fulfilled in one word: You shall love your neighbor as yourself."

DAY #7 : SILENCE

Duet 8:2 (NIV)
"Remember how the Lord your God led you in wilderness these 40 yrs, to humble and test you in order to know what was in your heart, whether or not you would keep his commands."

Lamentations 3:25 (ESV)
"The Lord is good to those who wait for him, to the soul who seeks him."

Lamentations 3:25-28 (CEV)
"The Lord is kind to everyone who trusts and obey him. It is good to wait patiently for the Lord to save us. When we are young, it is good to struggle hard and to sit silently alone, if this is what the Lord intends."

Matthew 4:1 (ESV)
"Then Jesus was led up by the Spirit into the wilderness to be tempted by the Devil."

Psalm 27:13-14 (NIV)
"I remain confident of this; I will see the goodness of the Lord in the land of the living. Wait for the Lord; be strong and take heart and wait for the Lord."

Hebrews 11:1 (NLT)
"Faith is the confidence that what we hope for will actually happen; it gives us assurance about things we cannot see."

1 Peter 4:12-13 (MSG)
"Friends, when life gets really difficult, don't jump to the conclusion that God isn't on the job. Instead, be glad that you are in the very thick of what Christ experienced. This is a spiritual refining process, with glory just around the corner."

DAY #8 : FAITHFUL

I Corinthians 15:58 (CEV)
"My dear friends, stand firm and don't be shaken. Always keep busy working for the Lord. You know that everything you do for him is worthwhile."

Colossians 2:6-7 (CEV)
"You have accepted Christ Jesus as your Lord. Now keep on following him. Plant your roots in Christ and let him be the foundation for your life. Be strong in your faith, just as you were taught. And be grateful."

Isaiah 26:3 (CEV)
"The Lord gives perfect peace to those whose faith is firm."

Jeremiah 17:7-8 (CEV)
"But I will bless those who trust me, the Lord. They will be like trees growing beside a stream – trees with roots that reach down to the water, and with leaves that are always green. They bear fruit every ear and are never worried by a lack of rain."

Habakkuk 2:4b (MSG)
"But the person in right standing before God through loyal and steady believing is fully alive, really alive."

Matthew 9:29 (NIV)
"Then he touched their eyes and said, 'According to your faith let it be done to you."

2 Timothy 4:7-8 (NLT)
"I have fought the good fight, I have finished the race, and I have remained faithful. And now the prize awaits me – the crown of righteousness, which the Lord, the righteous Judge, will give me on the day of his return."

James 2:14 (CEV)
"My friends, what good is it to say you have faith, when you don't do anything to show you really do have faith? Can this kind of faith save you?"

Mark 6:5-6 (CEV)
"Jesus could not work any miracles there, except to heal a few sick people by placing his hands on the. He was surprised that the people did not have any faith."

DAY #9 : GUIDE

Isaiah 58:11 (CEV)
"The Lord will always guide you and provide good things to eat when you are in the desert. He will make you healthy. You will be like a garden that has plenty of water or like a stream that never runs dry."

Psalm 32:8 (NIV)
"I will instruct you and teach you in the way you should go; I will guide you with my eye."

Isaiah 28:23-26, 29 (NIV)
"Listen and hear my voice; pay attention and hear what I say. When a farmer plows for planting, does he plow continually? Does he keep on breaking up and working the soil? When he has leveled the surface, does he not sow caraway and scatter cumin? Does he not plant wheat in its place, barley in its plot, and spelt in its field? His God instructs him and teaches him the right way... All this also comes from the Lord Almighty, whose plan is wonderful, whose wisdom is magnificent."

Psalm 143:10 (CEV)
"You are my God. Show me what you want me to do, and let your gentle Spirit lead me in the right path."

John 14:26 (CEV)
"But the Holy Spirit will come and help you, because the Father will send the Spirit to take my place. The Spirit will teach you everything and will remind you of what I said while I was with you."

John 16:13 (NIV)
"But when he, the Spirit of truth, comes, he will guide you into all the truth. He will not speak on his own; he will speak only what he hears, and he will tell you what is yet to come."

Numbers 9:15-23 (CEV)
"As soon as the sacred tent was set up, a thick cloud appeared and covered it. The cloud was there each day, and during the night, a fire could be seen in it. The Lord used this cloud to tell the Israelites when to move their camp and where to set it up again. As long as the cloud covered the tent, the Israelites did not break camp. But when the cloud moved, they followed it, and wherever it stopped, they camped and stayed there, whether it was only one night, a few days, a month, or even a year. As long as the cloud remained over the tent, the Israelites stayed where they were. But when the cloud moved, so did the Israelites. They obeyed the Lord's commands and went wherever he directed Moses."

DAY #10 : OBEY

John 14:15 (NLT)
If you love me, obey my commandments."

Luke 11:28 (CEV)
"Jesus replied, 'That's true, but the people who are really blessed are the ones who hear and obey God's message."

Jeremiah 7:23 (ESV)
"But this command I gave them: 'Obey my voice, and I will be your God, and you shall be my people. And walk in all the way that I command you, that it may be well with you.'"

Psalm 97:11-12 (CEV)
"If you obey and do right, a light will show you the way and fill you with happiness. You are the Lord's people! So celebrate and praise the only God."

Isaiah 30:1-3 (ESV)
"'Ah, stubborn children,' declares the Lord, 'who carry out a plan, but not mine, and who make an alliance, but not of my Spirit, that they may add sin to sin; who set out to go down to Egypt, without asking for my direction, to take refuge in the protection of Pharaoh and to seek shelter in the shadow of Egypt! Therefore shall the protection of Pharoah turn to your shame, and the shelter in the shadow of Egypt to your humiliation."

Hebrews 3:7-11, 18 (ESV)
"Therefore, as the Holy Spirit says, "Today, if you hear his voice, do not harden your hearts as in the rebellion, on the day of testing in the wilderness, where your fathers put me to the test and saw my works for forty years. Therefore I was provoked with that generation, and said, 'They always go astray in their heart; they have not known my ways.' As I swore in my wrath, 'They shall not

enter my rest... And to whom did he swear that they would not enter his rest, but to those who were disobedient?"

Galatians 6:7-8 (CEV)
"You cannot fool God, so don't make a fool of yourself! You will harvest what you plant. If you follow your selfish desires, you will harvest destruction, but if you follow the Spirit, you will harvest eternal life."

DAY #11 : HOPE

Psalm 27:13 (NIV)
"I remain confidant of this; I will see the goodness of the Lord in the land of the living. Wait for the Lord; Be strong and take heart and wait for the Lord"

1 Corinthians 2:9 (CEV)
"But it is just as the Scriptures say, 'What God has planned for people who love him is more than eyes have seen or ears have heard. It has never even entered our minds!"

Isaiah 55:9 (NLT)
"'My thoughts are nothing like your thoughts,' says the Lord. 'And my ways are far beyond anything you could imagine. For just as the heavens are higher than the earth, so my ways are higher than your thoughts."

Ephesians 3:20 (NIV)
"Now to him who is able to do immeasurably more than all we ask or imagine, according to his power that is at work within us, to him be glory in the church and in Christ Jesus throughout all generations, for ever and ever! Amen."

Proverbs 19:21 (ESV)
"Many are the plans in the mind of a man, but it is the purpose of the Lord that will stand."

Job 42:2 (ESV)
"I know that you can do all things, and that no purpose of yours can be thwarted."

Psalm 138:8 (ESV)
"The Lord will fulfill His purpose for me; your steadfast love, O Lord, endures forever. Do not forsake the work of your hands."

Ephesians 1:18-20 (NIV)

"I pray that the eyes of your heart may be enlightened in order that you may know the hope to which he has called you, the riches of his glorious inheritance in his holy people, and his incomparably great power for us who believe. That power is the same as the mighty strength he exerted when he raised Christ from the dead and seated him at his right hand in the heavenly realms, far above all rule and authority, power and dominion, and every name that is invoked, not only in the present age but also in the one to come."

DAY #12 : HEAVENLY

2 Corinthians 4:18 (NIV)

"So we fix our eyes not on what is seen, but what is unseen, since what is seen is temporary, but what is unseen is eternal."

Colossians 3:1-3 (NIV)

"Since, then, you have been raised with Christ, set your hearts on things above, where Christ is, seated at the right hand of God. Set your minds on things above, not on earthly things. For you died, and your life is now hidden with Christ in God."

Ecclesiastes 3:11 (NIV)

"He has made everything beautiful in its time. He has also set eternity in the human heat; yet no one can fathom what God has done from beginning to end."

Matthew 6:19-21 (ESV)

"Do not lay up for yourselves treasures on earth, where moth and rust destroy and where thieves break in and steal, but lay up for yourselves treasures in heaven, where neither moth nor rust destroys and where thieves do not break in and steal. For where your treasure is, there your heart will be also."

Philippians 3:20a (NIV)

"But our citizenship is in heaven..."-

2 Corinthians 5:1-10 (NIV)

"For we know that if the earthly tent we live in is destroyed, we have a building from God, an eternal house in heaven, not built by human hands. Meanwhile we groan, longing to be clothed instead with our heavenly dwelling, because when we are clothed, we will not be found naked. For while we are in this tent, we groan and are burdened, because we do not wish to be unclothed but to be clothed instead with our heavenly dwelling, so that what is mortal may be swallowed up by life. Now the one who has fashioned us for this very purpose is God, who has given us the Spirit

as a deposit, guaranteeing what is to come. Therefore we are always confident and know that as long as we are at home in the body we are away from the Lord. For we live by faith, not by sight. We are confident, I say, and would prefer to be away from the body and at home with the Lord. So we make it our goal to please him, whether we are at home in the body or away from it. 10 For we must all appear before the judgment seat of Christ, so that each of us may receive what is due us for the things done while in the body, whether good or bad."

Romans 8:18-21 (MSG)
"That's why I don't think there's any comparison between the present hard times and the coming good times. The created world itself can hardly wait for what's coming next. Everything in creation is being more or less held back. God reins it in until both creation and all the creatures are ready and can be released at the same moment into the glorious times ahead. Meanwhile, the joyful anticipation deepens."

DAY #13 : GREATER

Genesis 12:1-3 (NLT)
"The Lord said to Abram, "Leave your native country, your relatives, and your fathers family, and go to the land that I will show you. I will make you into great nation. I will bless you and make you famous, and you will be a blessing to others. I will bless those who bless you & curse those who treat you with contempt. All the families on earth will be blessed through you."

Acts 20:24 (NIV)
"However, I consider my life worth nothing to me; my only aim is to finish the race and complete the task the Lord Jesus has given me – the task of testifying to the good news of God's grace."

1 Corinthians 10:23-24 (NIV)
" 'I have the right to do anything,' you say – but not everything is beneficial. 'I have the right to do anything' – but not everything is constructive. No one should seek their own good, but the good of others."

1 Corinthians 12:7 (NIV)
"Now to each is given the manifestation of the spirit for the "common good."

John 6:38 (NIV)
"For I have come down from heaven not to do my will, but to do the will of him who sent me."

Ephesians 2:10 (NIV)
"For we are God's handiwork, created in Christ Jesus to do good works, which God prepared in

advance for us to do."

Matthew 5:16 (CEV)
"Make your light shine, so others will see the good you do and will praise your Father in Heaven."

Ecclesiastes 2:1 (NLT)
"I said to myself 'Come on, let's try pleasure. Let's look for the 'good things' in life.' But I found that this, too, was meaningless."

DAY #14 : IDOL

Romans 13:14 (NIV)
"Rather, clothe yourselves with the Lord Jesus Christ, and do not think about how to gratify the desires of the flesh."

Romans 1:25 (NLT)
"They traded the truth about God for a lie. So they worshiped and served the things God created instead of the Creator himself, who is worthy of eternal praise!"

Jeremiah 2:13 (NIV)
"My people have committed two sins: They have forsaken me, the spring of living water, and have dug their own cisterns, broken cisterns that cannot hold water."

Isaiah 42:8 (CEV)
"My name is the Lord! I won't let idols or humans share my glory and praise."

James 4:4-5 (MSG)
"You're cheating on God. If all you want is your own way, flirting with the world every chance you get, you end up enemies of God and his way. And do you suppose God doesn't care? The proverb has it that "he's a jealous lover." And what he gives in love is far better than anything you'll find. It's common knowledge that 'God goes against the willful proud; God gives grace to the willing humble"

DAY #15 : EQUIP

Psalm 1:1-3 (ESV)
"Blessed is the man who walks not in the counsel of the wicked, nor stands in the way of sinners,

nor sits in the seat of scoffers; but his delight is in the law of the Lord, and on his law he meditates day and night. He is like a tree planted by streams of water that yields its fruit in its season, and its leaf does not wither.In all that he does, he prospers."

2 Timothy 3:16-17 (NLT)
"All Scripture is inspired by God and is useful to teach us what is true and to make us realize what is wrong in our lives. It corrects us when we are wrong and teaches us to do what is right. God uses it to prepare and equip his people to do every good work."

Ephesians 4:11-16 (ESV)
"And he gave the apostles, the prophets, the evangelists, the shepherds and teachers, to equip the saints for the work of ministry, for building up the body of Christ, until we all attain to the unity of the faith and of the knowledge of the Son of God, to mature manhood, to the measure of the stature of the fullness of Christ, so that we may no longer be children, tossed to and fro by the waves and carried about by every wind of doctrine, by human cunning, by craftiness in deceitful schemes. Rather, speaking the truth in love, we are to grow up in every way into him who is the head, into Christ, from whom the whole body, joined and held together by every joint with which it is equipped, when each part is working properly, makes the body grow so that it builds itself up in love."

2 Timothy 2:15 (NLT)
"Work hard so you can present yourself to God and receive his approval. Be a good worker, one who does not need to be ashamed and who correctly explains the word of truth."

Proverbs 6:6-8 (ESV)
"Go to the ant, O sluggard; consider her ways, and be wise. Without having any chief, officer, or ruler, she prepares her bread in summer and gathers her food in harvest."

Luke 12:40 (CEV)
"So always be ready! You don't know when the Son of Man will come."

DAY #16 : BITTER

Proverbs 15:15 (CEV)
"The poor have a hard life, but being content is as good as an endless feast."

1Timothy 6:6-8 (NLT)
"Yet true godliness with contentment is itself great wealth. After all, we brought nothing with us when we came into the world, and we can't take anything with us when we leave it. So if we have

enough food and clothing, let us be content."

Psalm 50:23 (NLT)
"But giving thanks is a sacrifice that truly honors me. If you keep to my path, I will reveal to you the salvation of God."

Leviticus 19:18 (ESV)
"You shall not take vengeance or bear a grudge against the sons of your own people, but you shall love your neighbor as yourself: I am the Lord."

Hebrews 12:15 (NLT)
"Look after each other so that none of you fails to receive the grace of God. Watch out that no poisonous root of bitterness grows up to trouble you, corrupting many."

Psalm 73:21-26 (NLT)
"Then I realized that my heart was bitter, and I was all torn up inside. I was so foolish and ignorant—I must have seemed like a senseless animal to you. Yet I still belong to you; you hold my right hand. You guide me with your counsel, leading me to a glorious destiny. Whom have I in heaven but you? I desire you more than anything on earth. My health may fail, and my spirit may grow weak, but God remains the strength of my heart; he is mine forever."

DAY #17 : LAUGH

Philippians 4:6-7 (CEV)
"Always be glad because of the Lord! I will say it again: Be glad. 5 Always be gentle with others. The Lord will soon be here. 6 Don't worry about anything, but pray about everything. With thankful hearts offer up your prayers and requests to God. 7 Then, because you belong to Christ Jesus, God will bless you with peace that no one can completely understand. And this peace will control the way you think and feel."

Luke 12:29-31 (CEV)
"Don't keep worrying about having something to eat or drink. Only people who don't know God are always worrying about such things. Your Father knows what you need. Put Gods work first and these things will be yours as well."

Proverbs 20:24 (NLT)
"The Lord directs our steps, so why try to understand everything along the way?"

Ecclesiastes 5:18-20 (MSG)
"What is the best thing to do in the short life that God has given us? I think we should enjoy eating, drinking, and working hard. This is what God intends for us to do. Suppose you are very rich and able to enjoy everything you own. Then go ahead and enjoy working hard—this is God's gift to you. God will keep you so happy that you won't have time to worry about each day."

Ecclesiastes 8:15 (NIV)
"So I commend the enjoyment of life, because there is nothing better for a person under the sun then to eat drink and be glad. Then joy will accompany them in their toil all the days of the life God has given them under the sun."

Psalm 33:21 (NLT)
"For our heart is glad in Him, because we trust in his holy name."

DAY #18 : SATISFIED

Psalm 62:1-2, 5 (ESV)
"For God alone my soul waits in silence; from him comes my salvation. He alone is my rock and my salvation, my fortress; I shall not be greatly shaken. ... For God alone, O my soul, wait in silence, for my hope is from him."

Psalm 73:25-26 (NIV)
"Whom have I in heaven but you? And earth has nothing I desire besides you."

Psalm 107:9 (ESV)
"For He satisfies the longing soul, and the hungry soul he fills with good things."

2 Peter 1:3 (CEV)
"We have everything we need to live a life that pleases God."

Psalm 145:15-16 (CEV)
"Everyone depends on you & when the time is right, you provide them with food. By your own hand you satisfy the desires of all who live."

2 Corinthians 9:8 (NLT)
"And God will generously provide all you need. Then you will always have everything you need and plenty left over to share with others."

Isaiah 55:1-2 (NIV)
"Come, all you who are thirsty, come to the waters; and you who have no money, come, buy and eat! Come, buy wine and milk without money and without cost. Why spend money on what is not bread, and your labor on what does not satisfy? Listen, listen to me, and eat what is good, and you will delight in the richest of fare."

Luke 10:38-42 (CEV)
"The Lord & his disciples were traveling along & came to a village. When they got there, a woman named Martha welcomed him into her home. She had a sister named Mary, who sat down in front of the Lord & was listening to what he said. Martha was worried about all that had to be done. Finally, she went to Jesus & said, "Lord, doesn't it bother you that my sister has left me to do all the work by myself? Tell her to come & help me!" The Lord answered, "Martha, Martha! You are worried & upset about so many things, but only one thing is necessary. Mary has chosen what is best, & it will not be taken away from her.""

DAY #19 : RECEIVE

Isaiah 56:3b-5 (NLT)
"And don't let the eunuchs say, 'I'm a dried-up tree with no children and no future.' For this is what the Lord says: I will bless those eunuchs who keep my Sabbath days holy and who choose to do what pleases me and commit their lives to me. I will give them—within the walls of my house— a memorial and a name far greater than sons and daughters could give. For the name I give them is an everlasting one. It will never disappear!"

1 Corinthians 7:7-9 (NLT)
"I wish that all of you were as I am. But each of you has your own gift from God; one has this gift, another has that. Now to the unmarried and the widows I say: It is good for them to stay unmarried, as I do. But if they cannot control themselves, they should marry, for it is better to marry than to burn with passion."

1 Corinthians 7:25-40 (CEV)
"I don't know of anything that the Lord said about people who have never been married. But I will tell you what I think. And you can trust me, because the Lord has treated me with kindness. We are now going through hard times, and I think it is best for you to stay as you are. If you are married, stay married. If you are not married, don't try to get married. It isn't wrong to marry, even if you have never been married before. But those who marry will have a lot of trouble, and I want to protect you from that. My friends, what I mean is that the Lord will soon come, and it won't matter if you are married or not. It will be all the same if you are crying or laughing, or if you are buying or are completely broke. It won't make any difference how much good you are getting

from this world or how much you like it. This world as we know it is now passing away. I want all of you to be free from worry. An unmarried man worries about how to please the Lord. But a married man has more worries. He must worry about the things of this world, because he wants to please his wife. So he is pulled in two directions. Unmarried women and women who have never been married worry only about pleasing the Lord, and they keep their bodies and minds pure. But a married woman worries about the things of this world, because she wants to please her husband. What I am saying is for your own good—it isn't to limit your freedom. I want to help you to live right and to love the Lord above all else."

Matthew 19:10-12 (CEV)
"The disciples said, 'If that's how it is between a man and a woman, it's better not to get married.' Jesus told them, 'Only those people who have been given the gift of staying single can accept this teaching. Some people are unable to marry because of birth defects or because of what someone has done to their bodies. Others stay single in order to serve God better. Anyone who can accept this teaching should do so."

DAY #20 : SURRENDER

Luke 9:23-27 (CEV)
"Then Jesus said to all the people: If any of you want to be my followers, you must forget about yourself. You must take up your cross each day and follow me. If you want to save your life, you will destroy it. But if you give up your life for me, you will save it. What will you gain, if you own the whole world but destroy yourself or waste your life? If you are ashamed of me and my message, the Son of Man will be ashamed of you when he comes in his glory and in the glory of his Father and the holy angels. You can be sure that some of the people standing here will not die before they see God's kingdom."

Luke 14:25-33 (CEV)
"Large crowds were walking along with Jesus, when he turned and said: You cannot be my disciple, unless you love me more than you love your father and mother, your wife and children, and your brothers and sisters. You cannot come with me unless you love me more than you love your own life. You cannot be my disciple unless you carry your own cross and come with me. Suppose one of you wants to build a tower. What is the first thing you will do? Won't you sit down and figure out how much it will cost and if you have enough money to pay for it? Otherwise, you will start building the tower, but not be able to finish. Then everyone who sees what is happening will laugh at you. They will say, "You started building, but could not finish the job." What will a king do if he has only ten thousand soldiers to defend himself against a king who is about to attack him with twenty thousand soldiers? Before he goes out to battle, won't he first sit down and decide if he can win? If he thinks he won't be able to defend himself, he will send messengers and ask for peace

while the other king is still a long way off. So then, you cannot be my disciple unless you give away everything you own."

John 6:38 (NIV)
"For I have come down from heaven not to do my will but to do the will of him who sent me."

John 12:24-25 (NIV)
"Very truly I tell you, unless a kernel of wheat falls to the ground and dies, it remains only a single seed. But if it dies, it reduces many seeds."

Romans 12:1 (MSG)
" So here's what I want you to do, God helping you: Take your everyday, ordinary life – your sleeping, eating, going to work, and walking around life – and place it before God as an offering. Embracing what God does for you is the best thing you can do for him."

Matthew 26:39 (NLT)
"And going a little farther he fell on his face and prayed, saying, "My Father, if it be possible, let this cup pass from me; nevertheless, not as I will, but as you will."

DAY #21 : WHOLEHEARTEDLY

Psalm 9:1 (ESV)
"I will give thanks to the Lord with my whole heart; I will recount all of your wonderful deeds."

Psalm 138:1 (CEV)
"With all my heart I praise you, Lord. In the presence of angels I sing your praises."

Revelation 3:15-16 (CEV)
"I know everything you have done, and you are not cold or hot. I wish you were either one or the other. But since you are lukewarm and neither cold nor hot, I will spit you out of my mouth."

Jeremiah 24:7 (NLT)
"I will give them hearts that recognize me as the Lord. They will be my people, and I will be their God, for they will return to me wholeheartedly."

Dueteronomy 6:4-9 (NLT)
"Listen, O Israel! The Lord is our God, the Lord alone. And you must love the Lord your God with all your heart, all your soul, and all your strength. And you must commit yourselves wholeheartedly to these commands that I am giving you today. Repeat them again and again to your children.

Talk about them when you are at home and when you are on the road, when you are going to bed and when you are getting up. Tie them to your hands and wear them on your forehead as reminders. Write them on the doorposts of your house and on your gates."

Joshua 24:14 (NLT)
"So fear the Lord and serve him wholeheartedly. Put away forever the idols your ancestors worshiped when they lived beyond the Euphrates River and in Egypt. Serve the Lord alone."

Psalm 86:12 (NLT)
"With all my heart I will praise you, O Lord my God. I will give glory to your name forever."

Matthew 10:37-38 (NIV)
"Anyone who loves their father or mother more than me is not worthy of me; anyone who loves their son or daughter more than me is not worthy of me. Whoever does not take up their cross and follow me is not worthy of me."

Dueteronomy 10:12-13 (NIV)
"And now, Israel, what does the Lord your God ask of you but to fear the Lord your God, to walk in obedience to him, to love him, to serve the Lord your God with all your heart and with you're your soul and to observe the Lord's commands and decrees that I am giving you today for your own good?"

Jeremiah 29:13 (ESV)
"You will seek me and find me when you seek for me with all your heart."

Made in the USA
Las Vegas, NV
16 May 2023

72122949R00098